A Musician's Guide

to

Surviving the Great Recession

Practical Tips for Living a Truly Better Life in a Precarious Economy

by

A. Musician

For information contact: A. Musician P.O. Box 284 Peekskill, NY 10566

a.musician@theartistsleague.org

Print ISBN 978-0-9886746-0-8

eISBN   978-0-9886746-1-5

A Musician's Guide to Surviving the Great Recession

For everyone whose heart sinks
every time they open their mailbox
to find a pile of overdue bills.

And to all my artist friends — musicians, writers, actors,
illustrators, animators, film-makers, dancers, sculptors, puppeteers, acrobats,
jugglers, seamstresses and chefs - who've struggled, against the odds, to
pursue a life of art - and to live an artful life.

Contents

You Are, But Make it Work for You!)

....

ACKNOWLEDGMENTS

Love and gratitude to my infinitely patient and understanding friends and family, all of whom shall remain nameless, for reasons that should be obvious. You know who you are.

And thanks (and a scratch behind the ears) to A. Foxhound who pretty much taught me everything I've ever needed to know about life, love and the pursuit of Frisbees.

DISCLAIMER

While much of the advice in this book is a distillation of common sense strategies for surviving tough economic times, many of the tips and suggestions in this book could be considered, by some, to be ethically unsound, unsavory and even unconscionable. So I acknowledge at the outset that some of the survival strategies outlined in this book may be offensive to many and some folks may even consider them to stretch the boundaries of the law. The Author assumes no responsibility for any illegal actions taken based, supposedly, on strategies devised in this book. I am merely providing information and a personal perspective, based on real-life experience and observation, on how the world actually works. Ultimately, everyone decides for themselves what's justified in the name of financial survival. But if you find yourself in a quandary as to how far over the line you want to wiggle your big toe, here's a rule of thumb that can serve you well: don't be an idiot and don't fuck your friends.

Oh yeah… and don't get caught!

INTRODUCTION

There are two reasons you should take seriously what this book has to say:

1. **Musicians are *experts* at living on next-to-nothing.** Musicians, notoriously unemployed and underpaid, have always had to get by on less, so we're well versed in the tricks and strategies of bare-bones, economic survival.

   But, of course, sheer survival is not nearly enough.

2. **Musicians know how to live fun, fulfilling and productive lives without following all the mind-numbing, conventional 9 to 5 rules of mainstream society!** Musicians don't like to admit it out loud, but the truth is... we sleep late, we have more (and better) sex and we have *way* more fun at our jobs than most folks. Lawyers practice, accountants calculate, plumbers plumb, but musicians, well, when *we* go to work... we *play!*

CAUTION!: Some readers may chose to dismiss the above claims as outrageous and/or naïve falsehoods based on a commonly held prejudicial view of musicians as lazy, undisciplined, irresponsible layabouts. **Nothing could be farther than the truth!**
   Anyone who's ever observed a rock band pack up all of their assorted instruments and gear – guitars, drums, amps, stands - including sound system, into a van, then drive five hours to a gig, load-in, set-up, sound-check, perform four sets, break-down, load-out, and drive

another five hours back home (with a 4:00am diner stop for a bacon-cheeseburger platter), just in time to chauffer the kids to kindergarten, knows that musicians work harder than almost anybody else (with the possible exception of impossibly skinny dancers; though dancers still have less equipment to schlep around). And that doesn't include the untold hours musicians have spent since childhood, learning and practicing their instruments. Or the endless rehearsals necessary to further hone their craft and polish their ensemble playing. And not to mention the infinitely difficult task of composing or arranging or the dauntingly complex process of recording a CD. Doctors try to justify their obscene wages, in part, by arguing that it's fair compensation for the years of training they must endure. Musicians, most of whom start the lifelong study of their instrument at around age 9, just chuckle at that one. *The point is, if you're willing to cast your misguided prejudices and assumptions aside, all the other professions and trades, especially in these dire financial times, have a lot to learn from how the hardworking independent musician survives.*

. . . .

Tip #1: Think and Act Like a Multinational Corporation or Government (i.e. Lie, Cheat and Steal), Part I

The typical working Joe or Joanne is taught from their first paper route or waitress job to do what the boss tells you, follow the rules, obey social conventions and government regulations, keep your nose clean, or to the grindstone (or don't pick it), pay your taxes and everything will work out just fine and dandy... for your boss, corporate shareholders and the IRS, that is - not for you.

Sure, this system makes society *seem* to tick along very nicely... until that pink slip arrives, or you discover your pension has been looted, or a lifelong investment in your home has been wiped out by Wall Street shenanigans.

Curiously, while most folks sincerely strive to be conscientious workers and good citizens, we make heroes out of those successful individuals – CEO's, celebrities, heads-of-state, etc. - who, for the most part, tend to be the biggest liars, cheats and self-serving *assholes* in the world! Secretly, that trait is one we actually admire about them. How else to explain the abiding success of one of the worlds biggest certified assholes, Donald Trump?

'The Donald' is revered as one of America's most successful businessman. His books, like 'The Art of the Deal' were bestsellers, his TV series 'The Apprentice' has been a global hit. He's even made furtive stabs at running for President (God help us). Millions hang on his every utterance, enthralled by his supposed business acumen, thrilled by the sage wisdom of his stern pronouncement, 'You're fired!'.

In fact, 'The Donald', is just another spoiled, arrogant, self-important, rich kid, bully and thief, whose company, Trump Entertainment Resorts has gone bankrupt (along with nine affiliate companies, including Trump Plaza Associates, Trump Marina Associates and Trump Taj Mahal Associate) not once, not twice, but no less than *three times*, ripping off hundreds of innocent investors to the tune of millions, while extricating himself from any personal liability and walking away with a personal fortune. His billions in riches are the result, not of his awesome business savvy – his businesses keep failing and going into bankruptcy, ripping off his creditors – rather, his wealth is derived from his father's successful real estate business and his success in blatantly perverting corporate bankruptcy law to his personal advantage, at the expense of all the poor schmucks that invested their hard-earned savings in his ineptly run companies.

So, is Trump a true success? Or just a huge asshole? Or is he both – a hugely successful asshole?

And if he is, indeed, a hugely successful asshole, am I seriously advocating that you follow his example in order to survive these perilous times?

Yes! I am.

Now, I'm not saying you need to be as HUGE an asshole as Trump (that would be difficult, in any case, for most normal folks to achieve, as he's obviously blessed with a special talent for being as colossal an asshole as he is). But I am suggesting that you stop being such a goody-goody and a pushover. Learn how to bend the rules – or break them, if need be (but stealthily). Stand up for yourself! Being just a *little* bit of an asshole can make all the difference between whether you sink or swim in today's economy and the sooner you embrace that reality, the sooner you stop being a well-behaved worker-bee, the sooner you'll be able to take the necessary steps to work your way out of the financial hole you're currently in.

Am I proposing that you don a ski-mask, grab a pillow case and knock over the nearest Citibank? Definitely not (unless you've carefully planned out a foolproof approach, escape route and system for laundering the cash – i.e. don't get caught). What I am proposing is that you seriously consider the wisdom of emulating the strategies of some of societies most successful (and ruthless) companies, businessmen and government officials.

Here are a few more examples.

The General Electric company (GE), makers of everything from solar panels to jet engines to washing machines to the 'Tonight Show with Jay Leno' is currently the nation's largest corporation. In 2010 the company reported profits of $14.2 billion. (that's profit, not gross!) So, how much did GE pay to Uncle Sam in taxes last year?

Zilch. Nada. Zero. Nothing.

A. Musician

In fact - and this is where it gets even more hilarious (or obscene, depending on your point of view) – when GE filed their taxes, they actually claimed a tax benefit of $3.2 billion.

But don't criticize GE, they're just doing what all good corporations do – looking out for themselves. And so should you. Because as the venerable US Supreme Court made very clear in its 2010 ruling on the case of *Citizens United v. Federal Election Commission*, corporations are people too!

This is nothing new.

For years, IBM, which for decades was the biggest, and still today remains *one* of the biggest corporations in the US (indeed, the world), likewise, paid zero, i.e. '$0', income tax. Did they feel guilty about it? Not one bit. Of course, creative manipulation of the tax code is one thing, but collaboration with the Nazi's during World War II is another. For years, IBM has burnished its reputation as an evolved, benign, concerned corporate citizen. And yet, it's been documented repeatedly and irrefutably that IBM established its massive fortune by providing crucial punch-card technology and services to the Third Reich throughout the duration of America's war with Germany. The Germans may have gotten the trains to run on time, but it was IBM's punch-cards that told them how many trains they had and exactly where on the tracks they were. The only reason IBM's founder Thomas Watson wasn't imprisoned and hanged for treason was because the US Government wanted IBM's cool new Hollerith punch-card technology for themselves.

And while it doesn't nearly approach treason against the state, is anyone surprised to learn that Facebook founder, Mark Zuckerberg, was sued by ex-college classmates Cameron and Tyler Winklevoss for stealing their original idea for Facebook? While he may be heralded as 'Person of the Year' on the cover of TIME and hailed as the world's youngest, self-made billionaire for his visionary genius, it's pretty well documented that Zuckerberg swiped the whole idea of a group-based social network from two Harvard classmates. As is now well established in internet (and Hollywood) lore (and backed up by Zuckerberg's own emails), Zuckerberg was ostensibly working for the Winklevoss twins, programming their original new social website, Harvard Connect, while, instead, he was, in fact, deliberately stalling his promised delivery for weeks, until he had bought enough time to launch his own version of the Winkelvoss's idea, renamed, TheFacebook – succeeding in sneakily beating them to the punch. Zuckerberg has already paid the twins $65 million to put his light-fingered 'copy and pasting' behind him, but hey, it's no big deal, really. We're talking about a company with an estimated value of 50 billion dollars — give or take a billion (even after its disastrous I.P.O.). It's just business as usual, folks.

None of this is new. The history of the world is a story of people, companies and nations achieving massive power and wealth through murder and theft. It's how the world works. Indeed, it's hard to achieve statehood without wiping out the indigenous population and appropriating their resources. Hey, it worked for us! (And some would argue that it's still working for us.)

So, am I condoning murderous, amoral behavior, as a means of survival during this Great Recession?

No! Really, I'm not.

But the point I *am* trying to make is this... don't let the government, or your boss (or ex-boss) or teacher or parent hoodwink you into the naïve belief that everyone plays by the rules. They don't.

Successful people and companies break the rules all the time, or else they pay lobbyists millions of dollars a year to apply inordinate influence on politicians in order to legislate *new* rules, just for them – which is really just a clever way of breaking them legally, isn't it?

You don't *have* to be an asshole and a crook to achieve financial solvency.

But it helps.

....

Tip #2: Get Your Dog a Credit Card

IMPORTANT NOTE: Just because this idea sounds ridiculous, like some whimsical joke, don't assume that I'm not absolutely serious and that it's not 100% viable. I am, it is, it works and I've done it. Here's how it all started...

I love my dog. He's the best dog in the world. He can smell a pretty girl a mile away and, in fact, he introduced me to the beautiful woman who eventually became my wife. He's a great dog. And he has *better credit than me!*

Shockingly, musicians have a difficult time getting credit. Hard to believe, but true.

Bank managers roll their eyes when a musician asks for a loan. They can barely manage to stifle a chuckle when some earnest, long-haired musician politely approaches their desk and asks to fill out a loan application. Nine times out of ten it's an exercise in futility and the one time in ten that a musician actually gets a loan it's only because their mom or their girlfriend was willing to co-sign for it. My dog never had that problem.

A. Musician

A few years ago I filled out an order form for the Columbia Music Club. On a whim, instead of my own name, I entered the name of my dog. For the sake of anonymity (he's a champion frisbee catcher, but he shuns the spotlight), let's call him, A. Foxhound.

The CDs came in the mail addressed to Mr. A. Foxhound. Now, Mr. Foxhound is a responsible type (when he isn't chewing the sofa or ladies' shoes to bits) and always paid his bills on time. An avid music lover (his musical tastes range from pop to rock to classical with a special affinity for jazz-fusion), Mr. Foxhound ordered dozens of CDs, and over a period of time managed to acquire an impressive and quite eclectic music collection. Never missing a payment, he established a sound payment history and, lo and behold, one fine sunny day the mailman arrived with a bulky envelope addressed to one Mr. A. Foxhound. Inside was a pre-approved credit card with a $500 credit limit in the name of one, Mr. A. Foxhound.

I have to admit, upon seeing his name spelled out in raised, embossed letters on a brand new credit card, I suffered a momentary twinge of jealousy. How come he's got good credit and not me? He doesn't even have a wallet to keep it in. He doesn't even have pockets! *He doesn't wear pants!* My disgruntlement persisted; that is until Mr. A. Foxhound agreed to take me out to a fancy restaurant for a delicious three-course meal – his treat!

Mr. A. Foxhound reveled in his newfound credit, continuing to pay his bills in a timely fashion, and as one might expect, he began to receive more and more credit card offers, with increasing amounts of credit.

True to form, as the proverbial best friend, he never hesitated to let me make use of his credit-worthiness, allowing me to charge guitars, strings, cables, recording equipment and the like, or enabling me to cover the cost of hotel rooms on the road and to fill up the gas tank in order to get to my gigs.

At a time in my life and career when all doors were shut, when money was tight and opportunities slim, Mr. A. Foxhound's credit card kept me afloat.

I know I'm not the only one in the world whose dog has a credit card. I'm certain it happens way more often than the credit card companies would ever admit. And it wasn't intentional – at first. He ordered some music and they offered him a credit card. I just helped him sign his name (difficult to hold a pen with paws).

I finally drew the line when Mr. A. Foxhound received a generous offer for low-cost life insurance. Admittedly, I did spend more than a little time considered the intriguing possibilities, and might well have gotten away with it had I chosen to further explore the financial potential of my canine buddy. But in the end, I opted to leave well enough alone – and ordered a chromatic harmonica with my dog's credit card instead.

. . . .

Tip #3: If it Ain't Broke, *Whaddaya Need a New One For?* (But You Might Want to Bring It in For a Tune-Up.)

To quote Adam Sandler, I drive a 'piece of shit' car. It's got a huge dent in the fender from when my kid ran a stop-sign while staring at the GPS, when she should have been looking at the road. It slips a little, going into third gear and the oil leaks, but as long as I keep topping it up, it runs just fine. It's not pretty, but it gets me where I need to go.

We live in a fashion-driven, consumer-based economy, powered by steroid-enhanced innovation and planned obsolescence. Today's hair-style, hemline, flat-screen TV, game-console, reality-TV celebrity, hybrid-car or smart-phone app will be old news before you power up your solar-powered electric tooth-brush tomorrow morning. (Although I have a disquieting suspicion that Snookie will be with us for much longer than any of us dares to imagine.) Just when you were figuring out how to use all the features of the version 2.0 software on your smart-phone, they come out with version 2.1, chock-full of even better, more amazing features that you *just can't-live-without!*

You can! You should! *You must!*

An economy based on perpetual growth requires disposable goods. If we're not constantly buying new stuff, the system will collapse; which apparently is what's happening at the moment. (Am I the only one that thinks this economic model – perpetual growth - sounds suspiciously like an enormous global Ponzi scheme?)

Much as the corporate world (aided and abetted by the government) would like to convince us that this system of constant innovation and replacement is good and desirable and perfectly rational, it's pretty clear that unplanned, uncontained, unchecked, chaotic growth can be potentially devastating. For one, there is the abiding rule of unintended consequences. Cell phones are way cool! In this new millennium, it's hard to imagine life without them. But if the annoying teenage salesperson selling you your next smart-phone were to hand you a document stating that…

"Sound scientific studies suggest that use of this cellular phone device may have already led to the decimation of 95% of the bee population around the world (responsible for pollinating the majority of the farm grown food we eat), and oh, yeah, one other thing, we're gradually learning, based on non-industry sponsored scientific studies, that, yes, indeedy, you're probably going to get brain cancer on the same side of your brain that you use this cell-phone on. Coincidence? We're not really sure." Would you sign it?

I'm not a Luddite. (O.K., maybe I am a *little* bit of a Luddite.) Innovation isn't bad. It's just that unchecked innovation can be calamitous.

Aside from potential environmental hazards, this system breeds waste. I'm not talking about refuse, much of which can be recycled; I'm talking about waste in the sense of our not taking full advantage of all the potential use that last year's model still has to offer – that car in the driveway, those shoes in the closet, that three-speed vibrator tucked discretely under the bedside table… Spoiled by decades of post-war affluence, we tend not to fully appreciate what we have. Our current system of planned obsolescence and disposable goods dilutes the value of everything we possess and compels us to assume unnecessary debt in order to acquire unnecessary goods, even when we clearly can't afford them.

Take cars in Cuba. Up until 2011, it was illegal for Cuban citizens to buy or sell large-ticket items like houses or automobiles. The result was that vintage American cars - classic Chevys, Buicks, Fords and Pontiacs, from the 50's and 60's - passed down through families, are still on the road, today. Many of these vehicles, over half-a-century old, are still in pristine condition; patiently, painstakingly maintained by resourceful and inventive mechanics for whom obsolescence was not an option. And now, these so-called piece-of-shit cars, maintained by necessity, are worth a small fortune. Their inherent value as solid, reliable modes of transportation was recognized and nurtured, instead of their being junked for going rapidly out of style.

When things are flush, who cares? But when things are tight, value matters.

As a young musician, I started out playing a $75 acoustic guitar. I bought it at Manny's Music on 48th St. in Manhattan with a bag of quarters I earned on my paper route, delivering the Bergen Evening Record. I would sit on the basement steps (good acoustics) and flail away on my 6-string playing the only four chords I knew, writing simple pop songs, blatantly plagiarizing the Monkees, Herman's Hermits and the Beatles.

Eventually, I learned some new chords and evolved my own individual style, writing songs on guitar, and then piano, until one day, with a batch of self-penned tunes in hand and a sense of confidence and certainty far exceeding any realistic odds, I landed a record deal. Within a year I recorded my first album and six weeks after its release I had my first chart-topping hit single.

The hit single was a song written using the same four chords I learned sitting on the basement steps strumming my $75 acoustic guitar.

Since then, like most musicians in the last few decades, I've eagerly embraced every hi-tech musical invention and innovation in the ever evolving music, sound and recording field. Acoustic pianos were replaced by analogue synthesizers, which in turn were replaced by digital keyboards, which in turn were replaced by virtual keyboard plug-ins which could be installed into a digital-audio-workstation which itself had replaced multi-track tape machines. My first album was recorded in a major-label recording studio using 2" tape reels on a 24 track analogue tape machine the size of a VW Bug. Today, the same functionality can be achieved using a single microphone and a laptop.

Yes innovation is good, but here's the catch: every time a new synthesizer module came out, every time a new piece of audio software was released, I was filled with consumer upgrade-angst. If I could only add this piece of gear to my studio setup, if I could only afford this latest software patch, or sound f/x module, if I could only find the money for the latest upgrade on my recording software, 16bit, 24bit, 32bit... my next record would be so much better. I'd love to write and record something new, but I should really wait 'til I can get my hands on that new sexy piece of must-have audio gear.

I was caught in a vicious upgrade-cycle, constantly striving for newer and better stuff.

What I had forgotten, of course, was that all that technology was irrelevant. What *really* mattered were the songs, themselves. And all I *really* ever needed to write the songs was a cheap guitar... and a few chords.

It's a 'back to basics', 'make good use of what you've already got' theme that applies to every life endeavor. And it's especially useful when you find yourself with limited means. Figure out what's *really* necessary, what's *crucial* to the task at hand. Focus your energies on *that*; don't waste money on the incidentals, on the next compelling upgrade, on the extraneous fluff. Save it for something important. (Like buying some chocolate for your honey.)

This is a critical lesson that took me the better part of three decades to figure out. Appreciate what you've got. Make use of its full potential. If it ain't broke, don't fix it. If it works, don't throw it out. Embrace the concept, internalize it... and you can save tens of thousands of dollars over the next several years, money that can help you pay for those *really* crucial expenses in life — food, rent, gasoline and recreational drugs.

....

Tip #4: What Do You *Really* Give-a-Shit About?

This is actually the most important advice in this book. You can ignore every other stratagem and maybe, if you're lucky, you'll still survive this wounded economy and eek out a paltry living in some mind-numbing office-job. That's O.K. But, guaranteed, if you ignore this section – you're totally screwed.

Huh?

Here's the deal: musicians have one main, decisive advantage over most other professions when it comes to surviving in any economy, and it's this: *they don't really give a shit about making money!*

We may deny it (especially to our inlaws). But it's true. Sure, musicians care about paying their rent (unless they're living with their girlfriend or in their parent's basement). And sure, they care about keeping the electricity turned on (how else are they gonna power their amps, speakers and recording gear?) But what they *really* care about, what *really, really* matters to them…

…is the music!

You can't underestimate or dismiss the potency of these core feelings. It's a musician's secret weapon.

Because a true musician is so *fully* committed to the act, the idea and the lifestyle of making music, they are prepared to suffer almost any indignity, bare any burden, withstand any setback or humiliation... because in their heart and soul they know, with unquestioning *certainty*... that the music is worth it!

This kind of passion, this kind of total commitment is the *key* to surviving any economic downturn, while still maintaining your humanity and while still being able to remain – you guessed it – *happy!*

'But wait!' you exclaim, 'I don't care about being happy; I just want more money!'

Idiot! The economy sucks. You were born with*out* a trust-fund. Mark Zuckerberg is *not* your first cousin. (And the snot-nosed brat probably wouldn't lend any to you anyway.) Unless you're Warren Buffet or on the Board of Governors of the Federal Reserve System, you have absolutely no influence on our rotten economy.

But you can control how you *feel* about it. You can control the way you experience the economy by changing your perspective on it. By caring more about something else - something else *much more important* than money!

Hear me out! This is *not* hippy-dippy, flower-power, anti-consumerism bullshit!

Because here's the real kicker: if you're successful in doing so – realizing that other things in life – anything else... family, friends, art, nature, spelunking, bird-watching, your Boylan soda-pop bottle-top collection... the mysteries and wonders of life, love and imagination – are ultimately and fundamentally more important than money, the irony is that, having achieved that blissful perspective, you'll actually be better equipped and prepared to...

...make more money!

Look at it this way: It's like trying to score! If a young guy is *desperate* to hook up with that pretty new coed that just strolled into class, what's the best strategy he can pursue to increase his chances of getting her to go out with him? Simple! Stop being so friggin' *desperate!* It's one of those curious (but true) laws of the universe, namely, that often the best way to get something you really desire... is to cease desiring it.

It's that desperation which can be your biggest obstacle; it makes you nervous, self-conscious, less adept, less cool, less approachable, less likable. The more you want it, the less likely you are to get it.

It's an annoying reality, but the minute you cease being desperate, is when you'll find you're suddenly capable of performing your best, of being relaxed and charming instead of scary and off-putting.

This same principle applies to chasing after money.

Shift your focus, temporarily, away from the cash. Concentrate your attention on something you truly care about. Surprisingly, the boundless energy, incentive and motivation you'll get from doing something you actually love (ie. give-a-shit about) is precisely what's needed in order for you to seduce that lovely, sexy, big green wad of cash into your hip pocket. (Apologies for that disturbing but accurate analogy)

Only when you commit yourself to something other than (or at least in addition to) pure cash – whatever it is that calls to you - only then, will you be in a position – a dedicated, determined and confident state of mind – to move forward in pursuit of what you desire... some of which can reasonably include a bank account with more than twenty bucks in it.

Is this a guaranteed formula for financial success?

Nope. But it is a guaranteed recipe for achieving personal satisfaction, a sense of pride and self worth and ultimately, it's the secret to a happy life.

And that's a formula for *true* success.

You can bank on that.

....

Tip #5: Musicians Are of the Curious Belief That They Have a Right to Exist!

Some numskulls out there are bound to consider this a radical premise. Why? Because it challenges the prevailing concept of an artist's inherent worth in a market economy.

This book is focused on musicians' strategies, but I'm really referring to all 'artists', here; because what musicians have in common with artists of every ilk – dancers, painters, weavers, poets, jugglers, potters, architects, actors, beauticians, chefs, designers, writers, directors, animators, illustrators, etc. - is that their contribution to society is more often than not deemed 'frivolous' and ultimately 'unnecessary'. In purely financial terms, a musician's earning capacity in the open market is pretty damn close to the bottom rung of the salary ladder.

Society has decided – at this particular point in time – that finance workers, bankers, doctors, lawyers, plumbers and strippers… are entitled to make an affluent living; accountants, nurses, teachers, policemen, fireman, sanitation workers… are entitled to make a reasonable living; and that waiters, attendants, assistants, secretaries and clerks are entitled to eke out a modest living. *And that musicians (along with those fellow travelers – all other artists) are simply not.*

Society makes noises about valuing its artists, but that value is decidedly at the low end of society's remuneration scale. (Celebrity can be the one quality that does result in the artist getting generously compensated. But by definition, celebrity compensation is a rarity, a miniscule percentage of the artistic work force.) By any measure of comparative financial compensation by job description, artists – hardworking musicians among 'em– get the shaft.

Speaking as an artist. And more specifically as a musician… **that system doesn't work for me.**

A musician, like any true artist - or religious fundamentalist, for that matter – is absolutely convinced of their right, their *obligation*, to pursue a life of music as a full-time career. The majority of society believes otherwise.

The majority of society can suck my big fat dick!

O.K., admittedly, it's not that big; but they can *still* suck it!

With rare exceptions, the so-called straight working world has a big problem with the lifestyle choices musicians make. Annoyance born of ignorance and outright jealousy over a musician's seemingly wayward, irresponsible lifestyle, cause them to protest: *After all? Why should you – a mere musician – be entitled to earn a living?* And here's their flawed reasoning: *Look at the dumb choices you've made: you pursued a high-risk occupation that you 'love', with no promise of financial security or benefits like health plans or a pension. All you do is 'play' all day and night. You probably spend all your time smoking tons of pot and having indiscriminate sex with loose women!* (God bless 'em!) *Look at me!* (the straight world insists): *I chose to be a 'responsible adult' and take the safer route, hunker down and work a boring 9-5 job in order to provide for my family, like a real grownup does. I should be rewarded for my safe, 'responsible', no-risk behavior. You, a shiftless, lazy, good-for-nothing, irresponsible musician, should suffer the consequences of your risky career path. ;-)*

Consider this: As I write, US economic policy makers are toying with new strategies for allowing, not just individual cities, towns and counties but, entire *states* to go safely bankrupt, to escape the burdensome debt threatening to bury them – including the pensions promised to government workers. And speaking of pensions, every day, news reports are warning of the complete collapse of the private pension system, threatening the financial security, not to mention the peace of mind and mental and physical health of *millions* of hardworking people around the world!

*Say what? Yeah, that's right. It turns out that that supposedly safe, low-risk, 'responsible' career path that you - Mr. Responsible Citizen - chose, isn't so 'low-risk' after all. Turns out you (and not me) are going to be punished for taking the 'easy' way out. Of course, you could try to make the case that you were making the 'responsible' choice on behalf of your family. Or was it the 'cowardly' chicken-shit choice, because you didn't have the balls (or gumption) to follow your true-calling, be independent and fight for your right to earn a living while pursuing your life's passion. You weren't up to the challenge; you elected to avoid the **really** hard work of following the more difficult, unconventional path. Hmmmm? Which one of us truly deserves to make a living? The industrious risk-taker or the 'I'll take the path of least resistance' taker?*

Who's the lazy, good-for-nothin' now?

Well, folks, the real answer is – *both* of us should be entitled to make a decent living – if we work hard, treat people fairly and contribute something to society. And try to keep in mind, while you're desperately looking around for a scapegoat, that we've *all* been fucked by the *real* perpetrators behind this global financial crisis (the financial industry).

In fact, I happen to subscribe to the radical notion that I have a right to make *more* than a decent living doing what I love to do – making music. What's more, I believe – I *know* - I serve a useful purpose in society and deserve to be fairly compensated for it, at least as much as any banker, doctor, lawyer… but, truth be told, I'd also be more than willing to make less than a child-care worker, or teacher, or nurse… – because, frankly, they deserve the *real* cash!

The point is, if you're a musician looking for fairness and equity in the job market… you're not gonna find it. You're gonna have to create it yourself. *You're going to have to defy the status quo.*

And as any disenfranchised person or group throughout history knows, the simple act of believing that you are entitled to a seat at the table (as opposed to being left outside in the snow with the rest of the undeserving riff-raff, or hidden away in the kitchen pantry – if you're lucky - away from the worthier banquet guests) is the first step towards marshalling the necessary forces, attitude and strategies required to finally sit your ass down in that comfy cushioned seat – along with a full-bodied glass of sparkling wine and a half-rack of St. Louis dry-rub barbecue ribs – with extra sauce on the side.

If you're not absolutely convinced that you *deserve* to make even a *modest* living, you won't!

A real musician never doubts it for a minute. That's why we manage, *somehow*, to get by.

....

Tip #6: Be a Lazy Son-of-a-Bitch!

We weren't put here on Earth to spend 50 to 60 hours a week doing mindless, repetitive tasks like database entry. We were put here to live, love, eat, fuck, play, create, build, invent and look after each other for the very brief time we're here on this planet. Do you truly want to succeed? Cultivate your slothful nature!

People misunderstand the motives of a lazy person. They assume a lazy person has no incentive to do anything. On the contrary, a lazy person has more incentive than anybody because he so desperately wants to avoid what he considers to be needless, wasteful, time-consuming and unnecessary work, that he uses all his skill, effort and imagination to come up with some kind of crazy scheme that will allow him to avoid that unpleasant tedium.

That so-called 'laziness' is the mother of all invention! (Zappa notwithstanding)

You see, to a *lazy* person, their personal time is precious.

To be truly lazy is to commit yourself to finding practical ways of enabling you to enjoy your free time; and that takes skill, discipline, commitment and creativity to invent a way of avoiding a distasteful or time-wasting task.

Gutenberg's printing press, Eli Whitney's cotton gin, Thomas Edison's phonograph, Alexander Graham Bell's telephone, Vinton Cerf and Robert Kahn's internet (sorry, Al Gore) all came into existence because of their inventors' passionate, unyielding commitment to find a way to avoid tedious, mind-numbing, laborious, repetitive tasks! *Lazy sons of bitches, every one of them!*

In fact, if you think about it, Einstein was probably the laziest person of the past few centuries. How so? Because he didn't even bother to invent a single thing! Nope, he just came up with a slew of crazy, irrational theories about time and space which, in effect, enabled him to perceptually *slow down time, itself,* in order, of course, to give himself more time to hang out on his sail-boat, playing in the surf! [NOTE: he left the actual inventions – like the atomic bomb – to other less lazy geniuses like Robert Oppenheimer and his pals.]

Most people pride themselves (foolishly) in *not* being lazy. They're perfectly content to waste their lives doing useless work, for minimal pay, on behalf of their smarter and more prosperous (and lazier) employers. They've convinced themselves that their 'work ethic' is a virtue. A good thing too. *Because if they ever faced the truth about how wastefully they're squandering the precious minutes, hours, days and years of their lives, here on earth, they'd probably shoot themselves in the head.*

Don't be a dummy; be a lazy genius. Use your amazing brainpower, your indefatigable spirit, your boundless creativity (we all possess these abilities, we just have to unleash them) to come up with a perfectly lazy plan; figure out ways to spend less time at mundane work and more time home with your wife and kids, or planting bulbs in your garden, or playing harmonica or building birdhouses.

And here's a tip: when searching about for a plan or strategy or project or device to invent, apply your innate laziness to *'something you really give a shit about'*!

Because if you do, if you adopt this lazy approach, and fully commit to it, something incredible will undoubtedly occur…

Even if it takes you a year to realize your perfectly lazy plan, or ten years or twenty… even if you *never* succeed… in fact, even if you fail *miserably*…

It will still have been *your* plan, *your* project, *your* strategy, *your* ideas… *your* precious time and life's energy dedicated to *'something you give-a-shit about'*, something you actually *care* about, something that *matters to you*. Mundane tasks can be less oppressive, with the knowledge that you're doing them for yourself and not some idiot taskmaster. Tedious repetitive chores can be transformed into zen-like meditative rituals if their ultimate purpose is to realize your true passions.

And, strange as it sounds, by adopting this radical 'lazy' approach, you'll have increased your odds of actually accomplishing your goal by approximately 1000%.

And you barely lifted a finger!

....

Tip #7: Congratulations! You're Fired!

Don't panic. Losing your job was probably the best thing that ever happened to you.

You've been handed a pink slip. Your carefully cultivated career plan has come crashing down on your head and you're convinced that life as you know it is over.

It is.

And a good thing too!

Why? Because your conventional plan was boring as chalk and has prevented you from enjoying the best parts of life.

You see, there are significant, very real benefits to being unemployed. Musicians know this. Despite our disheveled appearances, we're savvy and canny and we know how to take full advantage of an unforeseen opportunity.

That pink slip? It's really your *golden ticket!*

To a new life. A better life. I life with meaning. I life of fulfillment. I life filled with adventure, satisfaction, excitement and fun - if you have the heart to embrace it.

There may be a few bumps along the way. Sometimes it'll feel like you're hanging on for dear life to the last car of a roller coaster. But it sure beats going around and round in circles on the Kiddie Tea Cup ride for the rest of your days. Strap yourself in and hang on tight. You're in for the ride of your life.

Because guess what? Wake up, buddy! This *is* your life!

Huh?

Oh, pardon me. I forgot. You're still in a panic. You're still dumbstruck by the certainty of impending doom. There's no way out of the mess you're in, so why bother trying to fix it? It's unfixable. All is lost.

Let me tell something: *It's even worse than you think!*

Really! You think your recent setback is an isolated incident? It isn't. You think you're alone with your strife? You're not. The entire planet is being buffeted by an economic tsunami that could take a decade or more to crest and recede.

So take heart. It's not just *you* that's fucked. It's *everybody!*

You're not alone.

Think about it… societies, collectively, around the world, will share the burden of our wounded global economy (with the exception of a few super-rich assholes), and by doing so, diminish our individual pain.

What I'm trying to say is, you really *are* experiencing a financial disaster and the sooner you accept that, the sooner you'll be able to shake off the paralyzing fear that it might actually happen – it already *has!* But *not just to you.* And you see, *that's* a crucial piece of information. Your current dilemma is a dilemma shared by a few billion or so of your fellow earthlings. And that means all is *not* lost. It means that some things about our lives will actually get better.

In a recession *stuff gets cheaper.*

Consumer goods of all kinds – from cars to catfood – have already become less expensive. Homes cost less. Apartment rents have declined. All sorts of appliances, furniture, jewelry, sporting goods… will make less of a dent in your wallet. Remember, when life sucks, it pays to appreciate the few positive advantages a deep prolonged recession will provide.

Some aspects of life will get slower, even as it seems other aspects are careening hopelessly out of control.

Fact: In 2009, as a result of the global financial crisis, world energy consumption decreased for the first time in 30 years, down by 1.1%. Less energy consumption means less pollution, which means better health and lower health care costs.

All of these phenomena are major inevitable shifts that are happening in our global economy that you can predict and anticipate and, if you pay attention to, take maximum advantage of.

Have you always dreamed of starting your own business? But you wouldn't dream of starting one in the midst of the great recession, right? Of course not.

Wrong!

Now's the perfect time to take your shot; rents are low, labor is affordable, goods are drastically discounted, services are dying for your business.

And if your new start-up business also happens to involve something you 'really give-a-shit about', you'll find you have all the necessary passion, fortitude, stick-to-it-ive-ness, energy, desire and commitment to get the job done.

But that's not even the best part of being fired. Here's what is…

You've just been forced to live your own life.

That's right; your precious time is now your own – and not somebody *else's*.

Business strives for efficiency, maximum output, increased productivity. Every thought, stratagem, system is geared towards exploiting every last ounce of your strength and every precious moment of your day in pursuit of their corporate goal.

That pink slip in your hand? That's actually a permission slip, entitling you to live your own life – not for some overpaid corporate executive who doesn't even know your name – but for yourself.

It may seem like you've just been fired.

Nope! You just hired yourself! Full time!

Now all you need to do is sit yourself down and negotiate fair and reasonable job benefits, which should include sleeping late, enjoying a leisurely breakfast, a daily stroll through the park, sitting down with a good book, practicing your guitar, fondling your sweetheart... But don't forget, like I said, make sure you fill your days with something you actually *give-a-shit* about, otherwise you definitely will fail, even if your long lost Uncle Dave dies, suddenly, and leaves you a million bucks in his will, or you pick the MegaMillions lottery numbers tomorrow. Do something you care about and you'll not only be a lot happier with less money but, paradoxically, you'll also be in the right frame of mind to make a whole lot more.

....

Tip #8: Those Lousy, Rotten M*&ther $@?#ing +%%&oles! *(Get Mad!)*

You've been screwed. Get angry. Get pissed off. Somehow, someone, somewhere took more than what was coming to them, and left none for you. And now you've been overlooked, sidestepped, marginalized compromised and dismissed.

Almost by definition musicians are constantly being ripped off; by promoters, by club owners, by managers, by agents, and worst of all... those miserable, blood-sucking, black-hearted, scum-bags – the record companies.

And yet, in order for musicians to survive we have no choice but to learn how to defend ourselves. And, in part, it's our burning anger that helps fuel our drive and gives us the energy and determination to do so.

But remember this: you may have been victimized, but don't be a victim. Because indulging in victim hood is a dangerous trap – it can rob you of the confidence, optimism, emotional energy and swagger required to overcome obstacles, navigate risk and achieve success. So, let your anger fuel your drive, but don't let it poison your state of mind and don't let it undermine your belief in yourself. The worst thing you can do is to waste precious moments dwelling in revenge fantasies and mental tape-loops of What If's and Why Me's.

Seriously, I'm compelled to reiterate this important warning: do *not* divert your valuable resources and energies by indulging in fruitless and pointless daydreams of kidnapping the head of your first record label, spiriting him off to a remote cabin in the woods, employing the subtle art of water-boarding (hey, it's not torture!) in order to extract his bank account details, using a wig and makeup to disguise yourself as him in order to empty out all his bank accounts, then injecting him with some hallucinogenic before shoving him out of a van, stripped naked with no I.D., in a dicey urban setting, thousands of miles from home... There, you see? I just wasted thirty seconds I could have made better use of making music, designing my next album cover or watching porn!

The point is: You got fucked. It doesn't make you a fuck-up! Just deal with it and move on. Keep your eyes open next time and don't let it happen again.

Use that anger. Cultivate that righteous indignation. Learn from it. Get better. You just graduated from the prestigious School of Hard Knocks. The tuition was high, but fuck it! Here's your diploma. Hang it on your wall with a 2" nail. Just don't smash your thumb into a bloody pulp because you can't control your anger and frustration. Remember, there are always more constructive things you can do with all that energy. Like hiring someone *else* to kidnap the head of your first record label, spirit him off to a remote cabin in the woods, employ the subtle art of water-boarding...

You get the idea.

....

Tip #9: Borrow Money From Your Rich Friends or Relatives.

Oh sure, I can see you all now, squirming in embarrassment and shame at the mere suggestion that you alleviate some of the painful, debilitating stress of debt, you're currently shouldering, by borrowing from someone better off. And it's not like you needed to buy, borrow or steal this book to figure out this simplest of strategies. But there is a stigma attached to borrowing that can be difficult for people without to overcome. (NOTE: Curiously, people *with* money don't suffer any of these qualms) So, let me see if I can help to eliminate some of the inevitable discomfiture I know some of you are feeling at the prospect of going hat in hand to Mom, Dad, Sis, Brother, Uncle Joe, Aunt Sally, High-School buddy, etc... when that jar of quarters you've been squeaking by on, won't even cover the cost of a peanut butter sandwich, let alone last month's phone bill.

In Shakespeare's lighthearted theatrical diversion, Hamlet, the character, Polonius, give his son, Laertes, this, supposedly, sage, fatherly advice: *'Neither borrower nor lender be'*.

Polonius was a fucking idiot.

The truth is: our entire banking system is based on borrowing and lending. Virtually all business is, and always has been, conducted using credit and loans. There isn't a single, king, president, prime minister, despot, CEO, CFO, galactic overlord that hasn't borrowed huge sums to get (and stay) where they are.

In fact, if you'd like to take a casual glance at our national debt clock http://www.usdebtclock.org, you'll see that the total debt owed by the United States government is rapidly zooming past 16 trillion bucks, with no signs of stopping anytime soon. That's around $50,000 owed per US citizen. Ponder that figure for a moment - if you're a US citizen, when you woke up this morning, you already owed fifty thousand smackeroos – over and above whatever personal debts you may have - and nobody even bothered to ask you if you were cool with that!

When it suited him, even the wise and penny-pinching, Ben Franklin, ignored his own financial advice against borrowing when he negotiated $2 million in loans from France to help the Colonies fight the British. If he hadn't, we'd all be celebrating the Queen's next Jubilee in Times Square.

During America's Civil War the US government incurred $2.6 billion in debt. To pay for the Second World War we went into hock to the tune of $269 billion, which seems like a drop in the bucket compared to the trillions we owe now.

And here are some recent corporate loans that should give you pause: $17.4 billion to Chrysler, $351 billion to Citicorp, $150 billion to A.I.G., $200 billion to Fanny Mae and Freddie Mack. Do you think the multi-millionaire CEO's of these companies were embarrassed, red-faced and humiliated cashing those humungous checks? No fucking way!

They felt entitled. Why shouldn't we?

The point is, if they're happy to borrow the big bucks, why should you feel any qualms at all about a couple of hundred or a few grand?

We ordinary citizens are conditioned to bow and shuffle and beg meekly and politely when we find ourselves in a pinch. It makes us more malleable, more submissive, easier to manipulate, more subject to accepting usurious loan terms, exorbitant interest rates, and outrageous conditions.

The act of borrowing can be depressing, humiliating and shameful, but it doesn't have to be. It shouldn't be. If you have more than you need, spread it around. If have less, you shouldn't have to feel like shit just because you're in a financial bind. There's no doubt that all those C.E.O's slept quite soundly while spending billions, *trillions*, of dollars of tax money that they, in fact, borrowed from – guess who? - *us!*

It's not always easy, but don't beat yourself up over needing to ask for a loan. If you need it – ask. When you're able… make sure you pay it back.

....

Tip #10: Give Yourself a Good *Kick*Starter in the Ass

Life on this planet is changing, rapidly, and at an accelerated pace. Old paradigms are falling every day. The computer revolution and the democratization of the internet is *real*. The silicon genie is irrevocably out of the box. You think this digital sorcery performs its magic with no consequences? We're experience some of them right now. And they're not all pleasant. Whole industries are being wiped out or completely transmuted and transformed by the addictive speed and malleability of a speed-of-light, information economy. Even inter-personal relationships are being drastically altered by new modes of communication and connectivity. When was the last time you signed your name at the end of a handwritten note? Or licked a postage stamp? Or sharpened a pencil?

But remember, dramatic change is also an equalizer. When everything around us is being transformed at break-neck speed, there's no reliable way to predict what comes next. And if no one can predict what's going to happen next, it means there are no viable experts.

And if there are no experts, *everybody's an expert!*

Including you!

And that's a good thing! It means you have as much information as everybody else in this boom/bust frontier global village. And information is power. And if you're smart - and sufficiently *lazy* - you can deploy that power to your own ends.

And don't forget, you have the crucial advantage of size. Small size, that is, along with the speed that comes with it. Old companies and paradigms are overgrown, stodgy and slow. You may not think you can possibly compete with the powers that be, but you're wrong – you can turn on a dime, you can constantly reinvent yourself, you can respond more quickly, more creatively and more effectively than all your old school competitors.

Not unsurprisingly, *musicians (and porn stars) witnessed this dramatic transformation before anyone else!*

How? Simple. Because of their manageable file size, music and pornography were the first two mass drivers of the internet economy.

Suddenly, overnight, anyone with a laptop could record an album, anyone with a video camera could shoot their own x-rated video.

The traditional porn industry saw it coming and made the best of it. Their business inevitably has become more decentralized but they embraced the new technological landscape and continue to squeeze every last titillating drop of potential out of it (sorry!).

The music industry, on the other hand, completely fucked up.

They were so aghast at the potential democratization of their gated industry - an industry already disparaged for eating its own young: recording artists, that is - that they began doing something even more insane - *they attacked their own customers.*

The major labels all got together and started suing consumers of music – teenagers, housewives, students and teachers – serving thousands of them with multi-million dollar lawsuits for the 'crime' of illegally sharing/downloading music.

Instead of acknowledging and embracing the novel new mode of music discovery the muddle-headed record labels elected to alienate the very music lovers that they depended on as customers.

The major labels have been in a nose dive ever since.

Independent musicians, on the other hand, figured it out fast. And made the most of it - by experimenting, innovating, taking chances and trying new strategies to communicate with their listening audiences.

Today, more musicians are recording and releasing their own music – and actually making money at it - than ever before. It's still not easy. Being an independent musician requires dedication and hard work, especially if, like me, you're committed to a lifestyle of extreme, unabashed laziness (see Tip #6); but it's happening.

Here's a remarkable truth: I make more money selling a thousand CD's direct to fans than I did selling a million units in the old-model, mainstream, music business.

This is, in part, a comment on the onerous abuses endemic to the mainstream traditional music business. But it also offers a glimpse into the myriad of opportunities our new web-based economy provides to fast-moving, quick-thinking, creative independent entrepreneurs.

Their business has been shrinking every year for the last decade. Mine's been continually growing.

Democratization in this information age is permeating every facet of society. And it's not just to do with easily downloadable content like music and porn. It's to do with connecting large groups of like-minded people together, online, independent of the traditional gatekeepers.

When Verizon recently proposed a $2 convenience fee, the customer backlash was instantaneous and impossible to ignore – thanks to the internet. Same with Bank of America's $5 debit card fee. The Arab Spring? Longstanding social inequities provided the underlying impetus but the internet played a key role in providing like-minded groups to coalesce. Does any question the critical role the internet played in electing, and then re-electing, America's first African-American president?

Our current paradigm shifts – a perfect storm of computers, the internet and globalization – have spelled disaster for vast sectors of the global economy. But, if you pay close attention, you'll quickly see that these traumatic changes offer untold benefits to anyone willing to jump into the digital sandbox and get their hands dirty with all these silicon-based toys.

You don't have to be a genius, or grad student at M.I.T., either. All you need is curiosity, some gumption and an internet connection.

Musicians gravitated to the internet, early on, because it addressed so many of their traditional challenges – it helps them reach their audience, raise money, promote their music and, crucially, it enables them to both warehouse and distribute their work, online, with virtually no overhead. These types of features are common to the needs of most businesses, but one – fund raising – is crucial to all.

Crowd funding websites like Kickstarter and IndieGogo have revolutionized the funding of independent projects, raising start-up funds for music, film, books, games, art and all manner of cutting edge inventions and designs.

Music CD's, films, animations, video games, board games, card games, concert tours, wifi sensors, 3D printers, solar-LED lamps, frozen fruit-flavored icicle-pops, vertical hydroponic food gardens... all of these independent projects have been successfully funded – some to the tune of $1,000,000 – independent of banks, venture capitalists or financial angels. A democratic social network via the internet made these new ideas, products and inventions possible.

Life, here on our getting-warmer-by-the-minute planet, is changing almost as fast as one of those wiley neutrinos from CERN's Large Hadron Collider. And it's worth keeping in mind that a single solar eruption could erase our entire digital infrastructure in an instant (hold on to those vinyl records, if you haven't already sold 'em at your last garage sale). But, in the meantime, some things around here are getting a little bit easier. A few years ago, if you had a wacky idea for selling vertical hydroponic food gardens for urban windowsills, you'd be laughed out of the bank. Today, a small group of entrepreneurs from Brooklyn, doing just that, have raised $257,307 from 1,577 individuals scattered around the internet via Kickstarter's crowd-funding website. And they didn't even have to surrender equity in the company!

A few years back, the futurist blogger, Kevin Kelly, posed the theory of '1,000 True Fans', the basic idea being that an indie artist (any creative, including artists, musicians, filmmakers, authors, etc.) would actually be able to make a 'living' if they were able to cultivate an audience of one thousand genuine fans, eager to support the artist's creative output and willing to pay a total of $50 a year for the artist's work. Kelly's numbers may be slightly skewed (in my experience, the real number is probably closer to 10,000), but the basic premise is sound.

Every day, more and more independents - not just artists, but entrepreneurs of every ilk - are proving that this model works.

The world economy and the technology it relies on continues to evolve at a rapid pace. Make the most of your advantages - small size, greater flexibility and increased speed.

If you keep moving you can pass your finger through a flame.

Stand still and you're liable to get burned.

If you can't depend on the old economy, get a good handle on the new economy. It's not coming - it's already here.

....

Tip #11: You're Not as Crazy as You Think!
(O.K., Maybe You Are, But Make it Work for You!)

In the original 1931 film, Dracula, one of the characters famously utters these lines, "They're all crazy except you and me! *Sometimes I have my doubts about you.*"

Never doubt the power and liberating freedom of being just a little bit crazy. By the way, just as an aside, any mental health professionals out there offended by the terminology used in this section, can do what Clint Eastwood's empty chair told Mitt Romney to do. Reason being, that my intention here is not to be politically correct, rather, it's to make some useful, salient points about human behavior. Also, the reality is – and you know this to be true – if you've somehow navigated yourself into the mental health profession, the odds are extraordinarily high that you're a total fucking nut-case yourself. (No use denying it; just look in the mirror and then in your own medicine cabinet!)

Just for the record, I'm not making fun of, or light of, debilitating mental conditions – serious mental disease can be tragic and is no laughing matter (Mr. Eastwood, a case in point) - the point I am making is this: various mental maladies and conditions have aspects to them that can actually help you succeed in significant ways.

In other words, a little crazy helps!

I'm not just being glib here, either. Nobel Prize winning mathematician, John Nash; author, Jack Kerouac; renown Russian ballet dancer, Vaclav Nijinsky... all were diagnosed with Schizophrenia. Albert Einstein, Sir Isaac Newton, Charles Darwin... all believed to have possessed attributes of Asperger Syndrome. Pablo Picasso, Thomas Edison, Thomas Jefferson... Cher (but not Sonny)... all diagnosed with Dyslexia.

Some might argue that these individuals realized their successes *despite* their mental challenges, but many more are convinced that it was, in large part, these mental challenges that provided them with the unique perspective enabling them to succeed so dramatically in their respective fields.

More than a few authors have postulated that the vivid color and motion depicted in Vincent van Gogh's stunning art is directly attributable to a possible diagnosis of schizophrenia. It's easy to believe that the singular obsessiveness of Asperger syndrome might well have played a role in the voluminous cataloguing of a Charles Darwin. And recent experiments in dyslexia have proven that rather than being purely a deficit, some symptoms of dyslexia in fact provide useful and adaptive benefits, including increased peripheral vision and the ability to grasp the 'big picture' more quickly and intuitively when confronting otherwise confusing visual patterns.

Why am I telling you all this? Because, the fact is... we're all a little fucked up. Every one of us! And don't let any closeted cross-dressing, pill-popping, ax-murdering psychologist or social worker tell you otherwise! (Not that there's anything inherently wrong with being an ax-murderer, depending on whose head you're lopping off, of course.) And we're also conditioned to be embarrassed and ashamed of our peculiar idiosyncrasies.

Don't be!

Here's what I say: Embrace your out-of-your-fucking-mind, crazy-as-a-loon, mad-as-a-hatter self! Don't suppress the most interesting parts of you. And don't let anyone shame you into being somebody you're not.

People think you're a little nuts? Use it! Make it work for you. Use the gifts God (or Zeus, or the Flying Spaghetti Monster) gave you. Be yourself!

Following this advice will benefit you in two ways: (1) All that extra energy you've previously needed to *suppress* your odd tendencies will now be available and on-tap to pursue your actual goals, and (2) those very idiosyncrasies that drive everyone around you crazy just happen to be the most potent ingredients in your creative idea-generating and problem solving arsenal – once you liberate that craziness bottled up inside of you, you'll increase your odds of success by 1,000%.

Don't be a *total* idiot, though!

Craziness is powerful stuff and, as every superhero knows, from Spiderman to the PowerPuff Girls, *with great power comes great responsibility.*

Treat people right. And if you are gonna lop off somebody's head, be considerate - lay down a plastic drop-cloth to collect the splatter. Leaving a mess for someone else... well, that would be just plain inconsiderate!

A. Musician

....

Tip #12: Contrary to Popular Opinion, Parallel Lines *Do* Eventually Meet.

According to Euclidian Geometry 101, two parallel lines going off into infinity will never, ever, ever, ever… meet.

Because no one's ever actually visited infinity and returned to tell the tale, we'll just have to take Euclid at his word. (Unless you're willing to accept some flimsy mathematical 'proof'!)

However, in this case, I'm not talking about parallel lines in Euclidian space, I'm talking about parallel paths in our lives. Hear me out.

At least once a week, I receive email from an aspiring singer-songwriting, asking me to listen to their nascent efforts and politely beseeching me for advice on how to become a rich and famous recording star – like me!

First, I have to patiently explain that just because you're famous doesn't mean you're rich.

But then, I try to explain a much more important principle – the principle of *parallel paths*.

Almost every aspiring artist asks the same question – *am I good enough to pursue my music (art, dance, writing, design, etc...) as a career?*

The typical, and trite, response is, *only if you can't possibly keep yourself from doing so.* In other words, the presumption is that real artists simply can't help themselves – they're not really capable of doing anything else - they *have* to make art and they *have* to live the life of an artist.

While there's a lot of truth to that sentiment – artists *are* compelled to make art – I take exception to the idea that we're incapable of doing anything else. And as a practical matter, most great artists from Shakespeare to Charles Ives to Andy Warhol have managed to achieve their artistic successes while, at the same time, devoting considerable time and energy to the otherwise mundane pursuit of running a business – managing a theater, selling insurance, designing ads, etc. The reality is, most really successful artists possess the discipline and logistical chops to take care of the practical money making aspects of their careers, and in most cases they developed and exercised those skills before they ever achieved commercial success. Indeed, those practical skills played a crucial role in helping them to achieve their artistic success.

What I tell artists just starting out is this: follow a *parallel path*; pursue your art, but at the same time find something in a related field that will help put food on your table and pay your electric bills. Follow your bliss, but not blindly. Follow your heart, but use your head. Do two things at once: the *thing* you love and the *thing* necessary to pursue that love.

This advice is just as true for aspiring video game designers, business entrepreneurs, ball players, politicians, rodeo riders and astronauts as it is for actors, dancers and musicians.

Follow a parallel path. And here's the curious part - the part that defies Euclidian Geometry: Follow a parallel path - (a) what you love and (b) what you need to do to pursue your love - and one day you'll be amazed to discover that those very skills that you developed pursuing the more mundane, tedious, practical, logistical path turn out to be invaluable skills when pursuing your true passion! Your parallel paths have converged! The discipline, the organizational skills, the social and political skills, the work ethic... all those attributes will make you a better artist, musician, inventor, designer, teacher, scientist, sculptor, cop, banker, surfer, baker and journalist. Life's choices are seldom either/or. The idea that you have to devote yourself 100% to a chosen path is a false choice. Follow a parallel path. Find balance between what you want to do and what you have to do in order to make it happen. You'll find life is more interesting, more of an adventure. And at the end of the day, you'll likely discover that some of those things you once considered to be tedious, boring and mundane are, in fact, fascinating and fun; while some aspects of those dreams and fantasies of success that you had, that drove you for so long and for so far, may turn out to be not quite as amazing or wonderful as you'd once imagined. Life's funny that way.

The important thing to remember, though, is that *you don't have to chose between being practical and taking a chance* – do both!

....

Tip #13: Fuck 'Em! Don't Pay Your Bills!

This chapter is guaranteed to make TV personality and personal finance guru, Suze Orman, split a gut. Good! So, pay attention…

A guiding principle of this book is to copy the behavior of the big guys – you know, the folks with money: corporations, governments and rich assholes like Donald Trump. How do you think they wound up accumulating all their power and resources in the first place? By stiffing the little guy, that's how. Governments steal land and all the resources on it. Corporations go bankrupt leaving financial devastation in their wake. The Donald has gone bankrupt not once, not twice, not three times, but four times in just the last decade. The spoiled billionaire blowhard has been quoted, "I've used the laws of this country to pare debt… We'll make a fantastic deal. You know, it's like on 'The Apprentice.' It's not personal. It's just business." Remember that: 'It's just business.' (Wait a minute… didn't Don Corleone say that in the Godfather?)

The Taj Mahal, Trump Plaza, Trump Hotels and Casino Resorts Inc., Trump Entertainment Resorts - the eponymous crown jewels of this self-promoting dufus; each of these businesses was driven into bankruptcy when the comb-over king's renown business acumen sunk them billions of dollars into debt.

And just who do you think got left holding the bag, forced to pay the price for Trumps bloated delusional folly? It shouldn't surprise you: most of the debt Trump incurred was through bonds that had been sold to the public. That's right ordinary hardworking Joes. Life savings were lost. Retirement funds decimated. They got fucked and Trump walked away with the cash.

Now going bankrupt is never any fun. And it's not recommended except in cases of extreme financial stress. But, folks, in certain situations, when the shit really hits the fan, all sources of revenue are tapped out and debt collectors are banging down the door, your phone ringing off the hook... declaring bankruptcy can sometimes be a very viable option.

Worried about your credit rating? That's a valid concern. Good credit is a really nice thing to have. It's worth striving for, and well worth maintaining, once you have it. But sometimes, now matter how hard you try, no matter how disciplined you've been, no matter how noble or well behaved a citizen you've been, you can find yourself falling far, far behind.

There may come a point, no matter how vigorously you've fought to avoid it, that your credit rating is going to take a hit.

Don't cry.

Because here's the thing... Here's a terrible secret the world hopes you'll never learn: Having *bad credit...* can be incredibly liberating!

Huh? It's true. I know I'm going to get shit for this but here goes: Avoid it if you can, but if it happens, anyway, despite your best efforts, once you're credit rating has been seriously damaged, *you can stop worrying about paying all those bills on time!*

It's kinda like getting a dent on your brand new car. Once you've had that first little fender-bender, the next ding won't be quite as traumatic.

Pay off your heating fuel bills a little bit at a time. They'll send annoying letters and call during dinner, but who cares? Change your phone number. Change your name! The phone bill, utilities? Tell 'em you just moved in and need to open another account. File to get a DBA (doing business as) or better yet, incorporate and open a new account via the corporation. That's what corporations are for, to act as buffers between you and the world. That's how the Donald does it! Why not you?

It's possible to avoid thousands of dollars in phone, utility (and other) bills by simply switching providers while opening accounts under a new name – and get away with it! Is this ethical? I don't know; is it ethical for the phone company to over charge you for internet connection fees, or data charges over your impossible to understand monthly limits? Is it ethical for the CEO's of local power companies to constantly raise rates, when they continue to enjoy an effective monopoly, while paying themselves million dollar salaries and bonuses? Is it ethical for a hospital to charge you $25,000 for a half-hour surgery and an overnight hospital stay?

Bill collectors can be a nuisance, but you'd be surprised at how many simply give up after a while, if they become convinced that they'll never get paid. Consider this: have you ever tried to get a promised refund back from a major corporation or a necessary medical procedure or household damage claim covered by your insurance company? They'll keep you hanging on the phone for hours, referring you from one department to the other, ignoring your pleas, misfile your letters, refute and deny your claims... Major corporations make a fortune every year by making it next-to-impossible for an individual to collect on a legitimate claim. They know that if they simply set up numerous obstacles and stall for as long as possible, that eventually a significant number of people will simply give up in pursuit of what's rightfully theirs. Which the corporation likes, because now it's *theirs!*

Be like a big corporation. Drag your feet. Take a message. Be out of town. Be impossible to reach. Give them a taste of their own medicine.

And if, and when, they finally send the big guns after you... do what The Donald does – go bankrupt.

And they won't be able to touch you. Their annoying bill collectors won't even be able to bother you on the phone anymore. It can even put a temporary halt to house foreclosures.

Supposedly, there's a severe social stigma associated with bankruptcy. Apparently The Donald isn't aware of it. Or he just doesn't give a shit!

And here's another one of those secrets that financial advisors like to avoid revealing to the general public: once you *have* gone bankrupt, it actually makes it easier for you to get a new credit card. Why? Because the banks know (1) you can only file Chapter 7 bankruptcy once every eight years and (2) most people only file bankruptcy once in a lifetime, making you a prime candidate for getting a new secured or even unsecured credit card. The interest rates will be high and credit limits low, but you'll still be able book a hotel, buy an emergency Valentine's Day present for your honey or order Tupperware online, while beginning the slow, painstaking process of rebuilding your battered credit score.

So, unpleasant as it sounds, be like Trump. He keeps being rewarded for his bad behavior, so why shouldn't you?

I would strenuously advise against the haircut, though.

....

Tip #14: Think and Act Like a Multinational Corporation or Government (i.e. Lie, Cheat and Steal), Part 2.

By now, you should have a clearer picture of my overall strategy for economic survival in tough times, which in essence is to emulate the appalling narcissistic and amoral behavior of the most powerful individuals, institutions, governments and corporations in the world.

This will sound unsavory to some, but the facts speak for themselves – with very rare exception, individuals and institutions in power got there by killing, enslaving, or stealing from, other people. I love the United States with all my heart, and wouldn't want to live anywhere else, but I try never to lose sight of the fact that this great country of ours was built on the graves of hundreds of thousands of indigenous people and that our early economic growth was made possible by the perpetual suffering of millions of African slaves.

Less depressingly, Steve Jobs, a secular saint to many, stole – or would you rather I used the term, borrowed? - the Apple Lisa computers' Graphical User Interface from the Xerox Corporation, after visiting their Palo Alto Research Center in the 1970's. Funnily enough, the supposedly brilliant, Bill Gates, then went ahead and stole it from Jobs – and called it 'Windows'. And let's not even broach the unpleasant topic of the hundreds of thousands of Chinese workers – many mere children - who work 80-hour weeks, suffering from depression due to dire working conditions and debilitating carpal tunnel ailments resulting from their jobs manufacturing, by hand, all our cool electronic devices like iPods, iPads, smartphones, notebooks, tablets, etc… Hey it's *business!*

How do these folks get away with it? It all boils down to attitude. Despots, corporations and government institutions may spout transcendent odes to peace, love and the good of all mankind, but when it comes right down to it they are universally arrogant and entitled, deceitful and duplicitous, wily and manipulative, thieving and murderous, and relentlessly unrepentant.

Again, let me stress, I'm not proposing that you go rush out to commit unspeakable crimes or knock off the local candy store for quick cash. All I'm suggesting is that you consider your own *attitude* when it comes to achieving your own personal success. You don't have to be or do evil to succeed (the jury's still out on Google), but it's worth considering that the folks who tend to make the rules, curiously tend not to live by them. And more than anything *it's their sheer arrogance and sense of entitlement that empowers and enables them to do the things they do.* They just assume that they have the right to do whatever it takes to achieve their goals. You don't have to behave as badly as them, but if you're looking to achieve some modest equity in this life, you'd do well to examine whether you even *deserve* to succeed in the first place! If you conclude that, well… maybe, just *maybe*, you *do*, you're already ahead of the game.

....

Tip #15: Dilly Dallying with Swiss Miss and Bahama Mamma – The Fine Line Betwixt Tax Avoidance and Tax Evasion (And How to Minimize the Risks of Identity Theft)

On his 2010 tax return, Mitt Romney (remember him?) reported $77,731 in "passive losses" relating to care and feeding of his wife, Ann Romney's, Olympic-quality dressage horse, Rafalca. Suddenly, my dog's credit card doesn't seem so preposterous, does it?

In 2009, an IRS report stated that 1,470 individuals earning more than $1,000,000 a year paid *not one penny* in taxes – legally! A good tax accountant, like a good auto mechanic, is worth their weight in solid-gold paper clips. And as you've already heard, that figure doesn't hold a candle to the $14.2 billion in profits GE earned in 2010 while not paying a dime in taxes, and, incredibly, claiming a $3.2 billion tax *benefit*.

They say you should dress for the job you want – not the job you have. Makes sense. I'd take it a step further: I say, pay taxes for the job you want – not the job you have. I want to pay the taxes of a multimillionaire. Hell, I want to pay the taxes of a multinational corporation!

And why not? The landmark Supreme Court decision 'Citizen United' declared that corporations can enjoy the same first amendment rights as individuals. Mitt even famously remarked that, "Corporations are people, my friend!". And a good thing for Mitt, too. Especially given how many of his hundreds of millions are safely stashed in Swiss bank accounts and soaking up rays in the Bahamas.

All perfectly legal of course! (or so we've been led to believe.)

Well, if what Mitt says is true, if corporations are people, if they can act, behave and enjoy the same rights and benefits as individual citizens, I contend the converse is equally true. People should be able to act like corporations and engage in the same kinds of evasion, duplicity, obfuscation, deception, sleight-of-hand and strategies for avoiding tax as corporations do. IMPORTANT NOTE FOR THE IRS: I'm proposing tax *avoidance* here, *not* tax evasion. Tax evasion is illegal, of course. A person (but not a corporation) could go to jail for engaging in such unsavory shenanigans. Indeed, a person could go to jail for even *suggesting* such a thing!

Heaven forbid!

When I was just starting out in the music business, enjoying the first flush of commercial success with a string of top-40 hits, my erstwhile business managers called me in for a meeting to inform me that they had, regrettably, neglected to file my income taxes for the previous two years, during the period of my highest earnings. Oops! Sorry kid. Putting aside the fact that I subsequently learned that they had used my tour expenses as deductions for their own tax returns, I was now faced with a huge tax bill and no means of paying it off any time soon.

After, first, dumping my management company, I attempted to

arrange a tax settlement, but every time I fell behind in payments, the IRS would put a lien on my bank account – and wipe me out.

The great comedian, W.C. Fields, having grown up in dire poverty, was said to have been so terrified of losing his movie career fortune that he supposedly opened up as many as 200 bank accounts all over the country, under wacky aliases like Elmer Mergatroid-Haines and Otis Criblecoblis.

This strategy worked so well during his lifetime, that it's estimated that only a quarter of the accounts – containing as much as $600,000 - were ever discovered by his heirs. Now days, most states have what's referred to as a 'W.C. Fields Law', which, along with the USA Patriot Act, prevents folks from stashing cash under pseudonyms. But it's *perfectly legal* to have more than one bank account under your own name or under a corporate entity. Which, just coincidentally, makes it that much more difficult for governments, liens, lawsuits and assorted creditors etc… to abscond with all your cash. One side benefit of this strategy is that it also gives you a slight advantage in the increasingly frequent instances of identify theft. It's unlikely that an identify thief will be able to successfully clean out a half dozen separate bank accounts at once.

You get the idea: many eggs, many baskets.

And here's the best part: assuming you've done nothing illegal - such as evading taxes - *there is a ten-year statue of limitations on the IRS's ability to collect on your back taxes.* If you behave yourself, operate as a responsible, law-abiding citizen, then, amazingly, after ten years… you will no longer owe that money to the IRS. True! (NOTE: the federal statute of limitations does *not* apply in the case of a false tax return or fraudulent tax return filed with the IRS with intent to evade any tax.

Also, the statute of limitation on tax collection for individual state taxes varies by state and some states have no statute of limitations, so you'll still owe any state taxes due.)

So, don't be a dummy! Be sure to consult a tax attorney, or a 'creative' accountant that you trust, for more info on the whole issue of taxes.

And don't forget – be like Mitt! Be sure to claim all those "passive losses" relating to the care and feeding of Fido and Fluffy. [IMPORTANT NOTE: Unfortunately, it's not quite as easy as simply deducting your pets' expenses; just like Mitt, you'll need to create a corporation for the purpose of exhibiting them or having them compete in some type of entertainment or exhibition or somehow demonstrate that they serve a legitimate business purpose. Guide dogs and therapy animals are viable deductions; guard dogs (Siamese cats? Peacocks?) are too. One couple who owned a junkyard succeeded in getting the IRS to allow a deduction for the cost of cat food after demonstrating that the cats rid their property of vermin, thus making their place of business safer for customers.] Be creative. Somebody's going to get all those deductions; it might as well be you.

....

Tip #16: Live Your Own Life, Not Somebody Else's – Hey, You're Going to Die, Anyway; You Might as Well Live the Life You Really Want to Live.

Notwithstanding the cryogenically preserved heads of past presidents, in Futurama, we're all going to die – eventually.

But let's not dwell on decomposition, putrefaction and rot. Instead, let's project ahead a few decades into the future.

First, consider your life now: times are tough, and you're struggling with having to choose between taking a supposedly secure, but low-paying, mind-numbingly boring, spirit-killing 9 to 5 job vs. taking a chance on yourself, going out on your own and trying your best to make an entrepreneurial go of something that you truly love (ie. give-a-shit about). You know what you'd like to do, but realistically the odds are against you.

You don't have to ask your family and friends, you already know what they'll say: these are precarious times - choose the safer route.

Sometimes we have little choice – if you're solely responsible for supporting a growing family, with little outside help, you're options may, indeed, be limited. I don't deny that.

But what I see proven over and over again, is that, way more often than not, we actually have many more options than we think we do. We just don't permit ourselves to consider them.

You don't need anyone to remind you of all the sensible reasons you should immediately abandon your unrealistic dream of going back to school and becoming an herbalist, or of building custom ukuleles, or starting your own line of musical ear-muffs, or constructing the world's largest toothpick as a local visitors attraction (hands off! I'm still brainstorming this one). You already know what they'll say.

It'll cost too much. It'll never lead to independent financial success and *cheese Louise!*, you're not getting any younger.

That's right.

Like or not, ten years from now you'll be ten years older – but you'll still be you. Except you'll either be the older you that long ago resigned themselves to the safe, responsible path assumed by most of us, or you'll be someone else – you'll be the older you that pursued your dreams, took chances, made calculated risks, had amazing adventures, suffered painful defeats and enjoyed sweet triumphs.

Which *you* do you want to be?

While you're pondering that crucial question, remember this: the choice I just posited is a *false choice!*

Remember, *parallel paths do eventually meet!* I repeat: Follow your bliss, but not blindly. Follow your heart, but use your head. Do two things at once: the *thing* you love and the *thing* necessary to pursue that love. Contrary to conventional wisdom, you *can* have your cake and eat it too. But, first, only if you believe that you're entitled to. And, second, only if you commit yourself heart, head and soul to working industriously, bravely, creatively, passionately - and as lazily as conceivably possible - for that mouth-watering, heavenly slice.

Life is ultimately inexplicable. No one can really tell you with any degree of certainty what path will surely guarantee success, and for damn sure no one can tell you how you should define success for yourself; not your parents, not your accountant, not your doctor, not your plumber, not your bookie – and for sure as hell not me! (Nope! I'm not offering refunds.) So, come to grips with this crucial truth. It makes no sense to live your life according to every one else's priorities, personal agendas, view points and prejudices. *Live your own life!*

Unless you're a die-hard Buddhist, you're not gonna get a second chance at living this life. And if you do, you're just as likely to come back as an amoeba or a porcupine or a mosquito or a shiny pebble on the beach. So, you might as well get it right this first time around - 'cause it's likely to be your last.

Will this philosophy allow you to realize all your dreams and fantasies?

Most likely not, and besides, from the looks of it, running a multi-billion dollar corporation seems tedious as hell; and you know perfectly well your spouse is *never-in-a-million-years* gonna agree to that threesome you've been fantasizing about.

But will this philosophy help you to live a richer, more fulfilling, more exciting and infinitely more satisfying life?

It's worked for me.

A. Musician

ABOUT THE AUTHOR

A. Musician is an internationally known recording artist with a string of chart-topping hits, TV and Film soundtracks to his credit. And, no, in spite of all those hit records, he's not rich – but he gets by. He lives in a treehouse in the wilds of NY state with his beautiful wife and too many squirrels to count.

www.ingramcontent.com/pod-product-compliance
Lightning Source LLC
Chambersburg PA
CBHW071020040426
42443CB00007B/873